CREATING MEMORIES

Making a memory scrapbook
for life's special
occasions

Published by Lansdowne Publishing Pty Ltd
Sydney NSW 2000, Australia

© Copyright 1998 Lansdowne Publishing Pty Ltd

Publisher: Deborah Nixon
Production Manager: Sally Stokes
Designer: Sylvie Abecassis
Photographer: André Martin
Stylist: Mary-Anne Danaher
Editor: Cynthia Blanche

Set in Weiss on QuarkXPress
Printed in China

This edition exclusive to

(949) 587-9207

ISBN 1-55280-169-1

IMPORTED BY/IMPORTE PAR
DS-MAX CANADA
RICHMOND HILL, ONTARIO
L4B 1H7

ENGLAND
WENTWALK LTD.
278A ABBEYDALE ROAD, WEMBLEY
MIDDLESEX, HA0 1NT

MALAYSIA
PRO ENTERPRISE SDN BHD
LOT 605, SS13/1K, OFF JLN.
KEWAJIPAN, 47500 SUBANG JAYA
SELANGOR D.E., MALAYSIA

DS-MAX
IRVINE, CA 92618
IMPORTER: #16-1241510
949-587-9207

CREDITS
Scrapbooking products from the
following companies have been used in
this book: American Art Clay; American
Traditional Stencils; Art Impressions;
Century Crafts; Chartpak; Clearsnap,
Inc; Delta; EK Success; Emboss Gear;
Fiskars, Inc; Frances Meyer, Inc.; Hero
Arts; Highsmith; HOT OFF THE PRESS
Inc; Marvy Uchida; Paperbilities; Paper
Pizzaz; Paper Reflections; Personal
Stamp Exchange; PLAID; Provo Craft;
Sakura of America; Stickopotamus; The
Adhesive Products, Inc; Therm O Web;
Tombow; Uptown Rubber Stamps; Z
Barten Productions.

CREATING MEMORIES

*Making a memory scrapbook
for life's special
occasions*

MARY-ANNE DANAHER

CONTENTS

WHAT IS SCRAPBOOKING? 6
What you'll need to know to get started — everything
from ideas to images and memorabilia.

ESSENTIAL EQUIPMENT 8
Scrapbooking tools including basic and decorative materials.

SORTING AND STORING MATERIAL 10
Deciding the best material to use and how to sort and store it for easy reference.

GETTING STARTED 12
Tips and techniques for creating wonderful and original scrapbooks.

BABY'S BIRTH AND CHRISTENING 16
Capture the magical moments of a baby's first weeks, the christening and the first smile.

BIRTHDAY 24
Make every birthday a memorable event, from childhood to old age,
by keeping an annual record complete with cards and other memorabilia.

SCHOOL DAYS 28
Capture all the good times (and even some of the less memorable ones) —
the achievements, trips away, social dances and other events.

GRADUATION 32
Celebrate this major achievement with a book commemorating the hard work,
grades and the graduation ceremony.

FIRST CAR 36
Celebrate this major purchase and step toward freedom and adulthood
in the pages of your own record book.

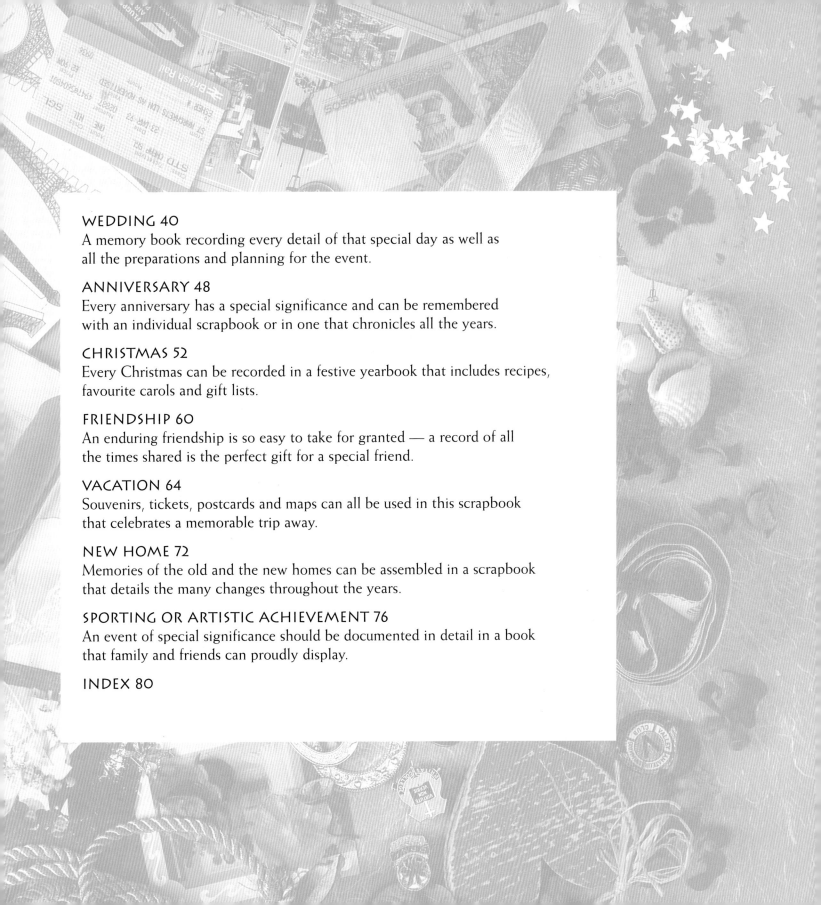

WEDDING 40
A memory book recording every detail of that special day as well as all the preparations and planning for the event.

ANNIVERSARY 48
Every anniversary has a special significance and can be remembered with an individual scrapbook or in one that chronicles all the years.

CHRISTMAS 52
Every Christmas can be recorded in a festive yearbook that includes recipes, favourite carols and gift lists.

FRIENDSHIP 60
An enduring friendship is so easy to take for granted — a record of all the times shared is the perfect gift for a special friend.

VACATION 64
Souvenirs, tickets, postcards and maps can all be used in this scrapbook that celebrates a memorable trip away.

NEW HOME 72
Memories of the old and the new homes can be assembled in a scrapbook that details the many changes throughout the years.

SPORTING OR ARTISTIC ACHIEVEMENT 76
An event of special significance should be documented in detail in a book that family and friends can proudly display.

INDEX 80

Scrapbooking
—a way to
**capture
memories**
in the making

Mementos can be used in a variety of ways in scrapbooking — to decorate pages or the outside of boxes used to store albums, or as attractive storage options.

Learning to preserve memories in inspirational and practical ways will not only allow you to chronicle the special events that happen throughout the years, but will also allow others to experience and relive these happy moments too.

Remember the time when ...? It is not always easy to recall every moment of life's landmark events, but with a little planning and organization everything you need to recreate the past can be worked into the pages of a scrapbook. A scrapbook gives a personal perspective on every special occasion.

Scrapbooking is a creative approach to making beautiful photograph albums using images, illustrative decorations and a range of craft techniques to enhance your photographs. All you need to get started are paper, scissors and glue, but there are many specially developed products that can be included, and archival quality materials will ensure your memories are preserved for many years to come.

A book that's been lovingly created can become a family heirloom that gives others an insight into the lives and experiences of their ancestors. It gives them a chance to delve into the fashions and social conventions of another time, to discover a long-lost cousin or perceive a family resemblance. Books such as these allow you to experience a specific event even though you weren't present or prompt you to recall memories that you thought had long since disappeared.

Many of us hoard items that have particular relevance to our lives, but often these are put out of sight and forgotten, only to be found again and discarded. Newspaper articles and notices commemorating special moments of historical or personal interest, childhood report cards, wedding invitations and birthday greetings are just a few of the items often retained for future reference. Materials that come to hand many years later can sometimes be slightly damaged or there may not be enough to fill a whole book. But with a little creativity these old treasures can be enhanced to give a wonderful, illustrated record of a special time.

In the following pages we guide you

6

through the best ways to approach scrapbooking. We give many examples of the impressive range of effects that can be achieved, using readily available craft materials as well as your own cherished mementos, such as photographs, letters, medals and ribbons, certificates, invitations, postcards and pressed flowers.

To keep your photographs and other precious memorabilia safe for future generations use only archival quality products — those that are lignin and acid-free. These materials include papers, markers, paints, glues, page protectors, laminating sheets, stickers and die-cut shapes.

For many occasions scrapbooks can be planned in advance (weddings, children's birthdays, anniversaries or vacations), but sometimes you will want to create a book of memories after the event, using the photographs and mementos on hand. Sorting and storing the photographs and other items will allow easy reference and are important tasks that must be done before you start working on the pages of your scrapbook. Good planning and organization will ensure a beautiful and enduring finished product.

Scrapbooks can be created in many different ways — in hardcover journals, with handmade paper sheets bound to form a book, or in ring binders with album pages slipped inside page protectors, just to name a few. Photographs and other precious mementos can be glued onto the pages and special items can be placed inside envelopes that have resealable ties and are attached to the pages. Quotes, recipes, poems, songs or other words can be handwritten, worked in calligraphy or cut out of contrasting papers to decorate the pages. The ideas are almost endless and will vary according to the theme you are creating, the purpose of the scrapbook and your relationship with the recipient.

So, welcome to the world of scrapbooking. Come and explore the ways in which you can utilize your craft skills and learn a few new ones. As you leaf through the pages many more ideas will spring to mind about how you can create your own unique book of memories.

Albums come in a number of different styles — post bound (to which pages can be added), ring binders (which can be filled with many pages) and bound, which are best used for special occasion gifts or projects that don't require ongoing additions.

ESSENTIAL EQUIPMENT

PUNCHED PAPERS

PAPER PUNCHED SHAPES

SCISSORS

PHOTOGRAPH CORNERS

GLUE

PAPER EDGERS

ADHESIVE

PAPER PUNCHED SHAPES

PAPER PUNCHES

Scrapbooking requires little more than paper, scissors, permanent makers, glue and photographic materials, but a range of other products can be used to enhance the pages and create wonderful decorative effects. The most important aspect to consider when selecting materials is to ensure that they are all of archival quality. This way, the completed scrapbooks will be lasting records. Archival quality materials will last for at least 100 to 150 years so the memories can be enjoyed by many different generations.

BASIC EQUIPMENT

Acid free/archival quality albums — three-ringed binders, post-bound and spiral-bound albums are the most popular.

Acid-free/archival quality album pages — for ringer binders.

Polypropylene page protectors — slip ring-bound album pages into these for added protection (use only polypropylene page protectors as others may cause photographs to discolor and fade).

Acid-free/archival quality glues — these are readily available in a variety of sizes.

Acid-free photograph corners — these come in a range of different colors and some even feature paper cut or printed decorations.

Acid-free mounting tapes — these are available in a range of different sizes.

scissors — it is best to have a range of different scissors for cutting paper — essentials include large sharp scissors and small scissors, such as curved nail scissors for cutting out shapes traced from templates or decorative details.

Acid-free papers — plain colors and printed papers in a wide range of patterns can be used as mounting boards for photographs, for creating die-cut shapes, and to form complete album pages.

DECORATIVE EQUIPMENT

pH neutral paints — there are many different brands of paints available, making for a great variety of colors. Use water-based paints and do not create solutions that are too diluted (washes) as these can remain moist for sometime and cause the pages of your albums to buckle.

Paper punches — these range from tiny to jumbo-sized shapes and include corner, border and other effects. Select motifs that

complement your scrapbook theme from the wide range available — everything from festive themes and birthday cakes to stars, squares and bears.

Paper edgers — select from the wide range of decorative scissors available and experiment with them to see them any different effects that can be created with just one pair. By reversing the scissors you will achieve a different effect easily and quickly. Use them to create fancy edges on your scrapbook pages, photographic mounting boards or use them to cut narrow paper strips that can be used as decorations on the pages of your scrapbooks.

Embossing tool — this tool is used to heat embossing powder once it has been applied to a stamped image. The heat makes the powder melt and create a decorative raised effect.

Archival quality ink pads — these are available in a large variety of colors and sizes.

Rubber stamps — there are so many different stamp images to choose from you are bound to find one which complements your scrapbook theme. They range from tiny motifs such as stars and animal shapes to large border designs

featuring flowers, swirls and lettering.

Stencils — choose stencil images which complement the theme of your scrapbook. Choose from the many different motifs available or create you own on blank stencil sheets.

Die-cut shapes — these precut paper shapes can be purchased separately or bought in theme packs that cover a range of different scrapbook subjects.

Archival quality markers — archival quality permanent markers are the only ones that should be used for scrapbooks as the colors will not fade. They are available with a number of different tips, allowing you to create wonderful effects on your scrapbook pages.

Templates — there are many available and they usually come in sheet form, featuring different outlines that fall within a theme, e.g. football, school, vacation. Ruler style templates are also available. Use templates to create interesting effects on the edges of your scrapbook pages, for tracing die-cut shapes and for creating beautiful mounting board for your treasured photographic images.

Acid free stickers and transfers — these usually come in sheets based on a theme, e.g. wedding, Halloween, festive season.

9

Collecting material for a scrapbook can be a daunting task, and deciding what to feature and what to leave out can take many long hours of reworking and referral. Creating beautiful scrapbooks will be made much easier if adequate time is devoted to organization.

It is best to allocate a clear space for doing all the sorting of photographs, cards and other bits of memorabilia, as these can easily become mislaid in the creative process. Designate a work area for scrapbook sorting, such as a large table or a desk, then set to work methodically. Sort and label all the photographs first. Once this task is done you'll find you have enough material for many different scrapbooks, and they will be much easier to find, saving time in your future endeavors.

SORTING MATERIAL

The first and most important task when working on a scrapbook is to gather all memorabilia and photographic material then sort and categorize these items. Photographs should be sorted according to theme — family, friends, baby, skiing vacation, anniversaries, birthdays, etc, then chronologically, starting from the present and working backward. Try grouping the photographs by year and create sub-groups by person, event or activity.

Make sure the photographs are correctly labeled for future reference and be sure to include the names of any people or locations featured making sure the answers to the who, what, where, when and why questions are clearly recorded. Label all the photographs with a photo-safe permanent pen, never a ballpoint.

Memorabilia can be sorted in much the same way, although many times it is difficult to recall a specific date. These items are best sorted by theme and can be safely stored in archival quality cardboard boxes or shelving systems, the outside of the box or drawer labeled to explain the contents. It may be useful to record all the items of memorabilia as you work to create a register of materials and their locations to make future reference more accessible.

Boxes for filing photographs are readily available in a number of different styles — you can label the dividers yourself to categorize your images for easy reference.

STORING MATERIAL

There are many different ways to store photographs and negatives but, most importantly, the originals should be kept in a cool, dark place in acid-free material to ensure a long life.

Cardboard boxes, shelving systems, paper folders, envelopes and hanging files are some of the alternatives available. Create a designated space to store your materials and set about making an ordered storage system in a spare room of your house, in a cupboard or under an office desk to make accessing the materials for future scrapbooks much easier.

There are even scrapbooking centers mounted on wheels or that come as desktop models, and these include drawers and files to store your photographs and memorabilia.

Selecting the right album for your scrapbook can be a daunting task, but it will be simpler if you keep in mind the purpose of the album and amount of material it will hold.

Three-ringed binders that allow pages to be added are more likely to offer the greatest amount of space, and page protectors can be used to encase the pages you have designed. Spiral-bound and handmade and bound albums are best for one-off projects and special occasion and gift albums, since pages can't be added to these. Post-bound albums are another alternative to ring binders as many of these allow extra pages to be added.

Use a number of different sized boxes for storing mementos, photographs and other souvenirs from special occasions. Set about filing photographic images and mementos as they come to hand to make working on scrapbooks in the future even easier.

Choose from the many different acid-free albums that are available. Ring binders are a good option for projects that may require future additions as pages can easily be inserted into these. Page protectors can be used so your work does not become damaged. Spiral-bound albums are great for special events or one-off projects, while post-bound albums can have extra pages added and are great for recording your children's developments and friendships over many years.

I LOVE MY NEW PUPPY

Creating scrapbooks involves much more than just choosing a theme and selecting images from your photographic files. Much care and thought should be put into crafting, decorating and designing the pages, creating the best possible album cover, the journaling that accompanies the images and the overall cohesion of the content.

After selecting a suitable album type, consider the cover decoration. Choose an effect that complements the theme — you may decide to use fabric to cover the outside of the album and decorate it using fabric motifs and embroidery stitches or use a combination of stenciled or stamped designs and die-cut shapes.

There are a number of techniques and tasks that need to be understood before the album pages are created. The following tips will ensure successful results.

Choose an effect that complements the theme

Crop images so any unnecessary background is removed to allow the focal points of your photograph dominate the scrapbook page.

Twinkle twinkle little star

CREATING A PAGE

Choose a focal point for your page — this will involve using a strong image.

Photographs can be placed directly onto the pages of your album or placed on mounting boards cut from contrasting or complementary papers to create an interesting background. Mounting boards or other backing shapes should be cut at least 1/2 inch (5 mm) larger all around than the photo image or they can be cut much larger to add extra color, patterned effects or add impact to the image. Mount an image on more than one mounting board, increasing the size and varying the color and edging effect of each mat. You can even mix shapes — place an oval mat on top of a scalloped-edged rectangular one or add lots of journaling to a wider mounting

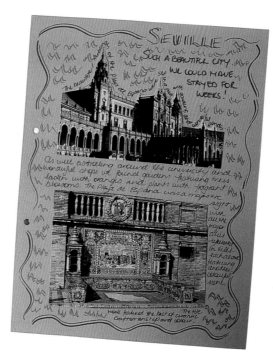

board and write around the photo to create a patterned effect.

Mix the size and shape of the photographs you have chosen for a page as this will create a better balance and allow one photo to become the focal point.

Collected objects can be included on the pages of your scrapbook — old and foreign coins, sporting ribbons, pennants and medals, lace from a bridal or christening dress, ribbons and buttons from children's favorite outfits, a swatch of your school uniform fabric. If unsure about the object's acidity, follow this pretty and practical tip to ensure the object and your album stay in perfect condition. Make an envelope from acid-free paper and decorate the front with words, a stamped image or a similar decoration to describe what's inside, or title the envelope "Open Me" to add a little intrigue to your page. Objects can also be wrapped or stored in a polypropylene protector page or wrapped in a small piece of this material.

Use the journaling around your images to create interesting effects on your album page — let the journaling follow the crop line of your photographs and write all the way around the image.

CHOOSING A PHOTOGRAPH

Often the image that will create the focal point of a page will be an obvious selection — it may be one which captures a favorite memory or is a very graphic or colorful shot. Don't forget the range of wonderful effects that can be created when ordering prints of photographs for your scrapbook. Sepia tones and hand coloring are just a couple of the techniques that can be used to enhance images.

Also consider what a photograph will look like once has been cropped — a seemingly ordinary photograph may create a much stronger image once the background has been diminished. Don't forget that one of the aims of a scrapbook is to tell a story, so select the image that visually says the most about a particular event and can be explained easily with accompanying journaling.

13

Choose complementary colored mounting boards for your photographs. A patterned-edged mounting board can be combined with a plain one to create a great effect, or combine different shapes to create impact on your scrapbook page.

If you have an overall coloring theme for the pages of your scrapbook, select photographs that also incorporate these colors or contain ones which complement the effect you are trying to achieve. Color, black and white and sepia photographs can all be presented together on a page or throughout an album, but you will need to use the backgrounds and mounting boards behind the photographs and a range of decorative techniques to achieve a good visual effect.

CROPPING

Before making any adjustments to photographs make sure you take a copy of all precious negatives and prints, then safely store the originals and negatives.

Once you make your photo selection you can decide how you want them to

look on the page. For instance, do you wish to keep the existing shape of the print or crop it to a more striking form, such as cutting around the image or subjects to highlight shapes, thereby drawing attention to them. You can use straight or decorative edges scissors for this, as well as templates, to create interesting shapes.

When creating shapes and cropping your photographs draw the outline on the back of the photograph first or on a paper mock-up before you begin cutting, as it's hard to reverse the process and preserve your photograph once the process has started. Use a light box to help align templates or other shapes on your photographs.

You can create interesting effects by cutting around the main subjects in a photograph — this is known as silhouetting. Use a sharp pair of manicure scissors — curved blade scissors are the easiest to use when cutting curves. Cut around the subjects and remove unnecessary background which will detract from the image. When placed on a plain or patterned page the image will now appear strong. You can also choose to silhouette part of the image and leave any special features that may tell part of the story.

JOURNALING

A photographic album will record in images a special occasion or event in life, but it's the journaling that accompanies these photographs that explains the highlights, capture the emotions, and describe the situation in detail.

Who? What? Where? When? and Why? are the main questions to address for each event, names and dates being the most important details of all. What to write and how to get started is often the most difficult part of the process, so ask others to record their experiences of the event on your chosen papers then glue them into your scrapbook to accompany the relevant images. Remember to create a balance of journaling and images — concise journaling can sometimes make a bolder statement and not every image has to be accompanied by an abundance of words. One paragraph of journaling may be enough to describe a page of images.

Allow the journaling to echo the shapes of the photographs, templates or mats, and allow it to flow freely around the image. Handwriting, no matter how it appears, will create a wonderful patterned effect on the pages of your scrapbooks. Write underneath, around and above photographs, using archival quality permanent markers, and select colors to complement the images or the theme of your scrapbook.

Lettering can be used as a great decorative effect, and using a range of different colored markers and writing or printing in a range of styles can add extra impact to a scrapbook page. Vary the size of letters and combine upper and lower case in words and lines, as well as the placement of letters, for instance, above and below the line or tilt the letters and words to create interesting effects.

Stickers can be used to replace the vertical and cross bars of letters, such as R, K, M, N, or can be used to replace the dots on lower case letters, such as I and J. Dashes and dots above, underneath and at the ends of letter bars or arms can also be used to enhance your writing.

SUE'S BIRTHDAY PARTY 1998

Different lettering styles can be used to decorate your scrapbook pages — use dashes and dots to jazz-up your letters, adding them underneath or at the ends of the vertical and cross bars of letters. Not all words have to be written in straight lines — alternate the letters of a word above and below the line to create interesting effects and use a combination of different printing and writing styles to make your pages unique.

FAMILY HOLIDAY AT THE BEACH HOUSE

This scrapbook page is decorated using fancy edged mounting boards in colors that contrast with the background. Punched shapes are glued in place to form added decoration.

FIRST SOLID FOOD

My mum bought me a jolly jumper and so I bounced up and down all morning. What fun!

Yum Yum

Mmmm!!!

I had my first big lunch today-rice cereal with pear. It was so good I wanted to grab the spoon off my mum and feed myself. What's for lunch tomorrow? I wonder?

Yum yum yum

Yum yum yum

Capturing the joy of a baby's arrival, the events and the planning involved in welcoming a little one into your home, are all aspects of a baby's birth that can be included in the pages of a scrapbook.

The amount of material you gather will require some careful planning if the book is to be a comprehensive tribute to your child and capture the many personal experiences associated with the pregnancy and birth. Start compiling the material and working on your scrapbook early in the pregnancy to ensure that no detail is overlooked.

When planning an album in advance and working on it as the birth draws closer, you should choose one that will allow the insertion of extra pages to accommodate the expanding nature of the project. If creating a scrapbook after the event, outline a plan on paper, allocating space to each different topic, based on the amount of photographic material and the number of mementos that you have collected.

Many mothers start working on their scrapbooks once they have confirmed the pregnancy. They note the progress of their condition throughout, recording their visits to the obstetrician, as well as the planning required for the baby, any renovations that are made to the nursery and the color scheme selected, special purchases and celebrations such as baby showers, and other memorable events that occur before the birth. Women often miss out on the precious photographic memories of their pregnancy because they're too busy preparing for the new arrival and don't make time to record their own developments. You may not feel very photogenic but after the event you'll be able to look back fondly at your pregnancy figure and think of a few wonderful captions to accompany the images.

No doubt there will be a time just after the birth when you will have little time to work on the scrapbook. Ask a friend or relative to compile a list of all the gifts and floral arrangements you received, as well as any professional photographs taken at the hospital. Label an envelope for each of the first weeks of your baby's life and use them to store mementos and hurriedly scribbled comments of your feelings and the

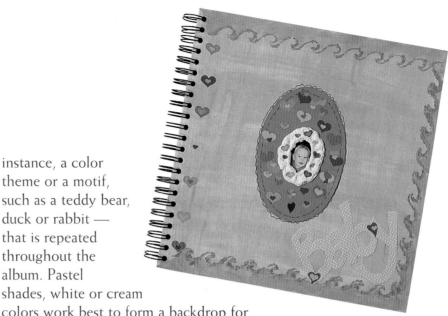

Combine stickers, die-cut shapes, stencils and a paper cast frame to create this pretty cover for a baby scrapbook.

baby's developments. Later you can come back to these records, elaborate on the details and transfer the material to the pages of your scrapbook.

Baby scrapbooks make wonderful coming-of-age or twenty-first birthday presents for your child — a symbolic change of custody can occur on the occasion to mark the child's transition to adulthood. You may prefer to start a baby album and then add pages to record other events in your child's life, or you may decide to make a number of scrapbook volumes — one for each year of their life.

Make a scrapbook for each of your children, so they all have a record of their lives to pass on to their own children in the years to come — a book that can in time be handed down through the generations and become a piece of family history.

When they are old enough to work with scissors and glue, encourage your children to contribute to their own scrapbooks and teach them the skills required to plan a book and design a page, so they can continue to work on their scrapbooks in the future or create their own books of memories.

Once the material is sorted and ordered, the next decision to make involves choosing a theme — for instance, a color theme or a motif, such as a teddy bear, duck or rabbit — that is repeated throughout the album. Pastel shades, white or cream colors work best to form a backdrop for baby photographs as they won't overpower the delicate images. Maybe you would like to select traditional colors, such as blue for a boy and pink for a girl, or use pretty pastel shades, such as pale green, yellow or apricot.

One idea for a cover design involves making a pressed cotton feature decoration using cotton paper pulp pushed into a terracotta mold. These molds are available in a variety of designs — there are even molds that form borders, allowing you to slip a photograph behind one to create a pretty framed effect. Cover the album with pastel colored paper, a beautiful piece of wrap that covered a gift, or paint it white before applying a wash of color to create a soft effect. Another idea is to use one feature photograph on the cover, mounted on a carefully chosen colored mounting board that will enhance the image. You may like to add a stenciled border around the edge

17

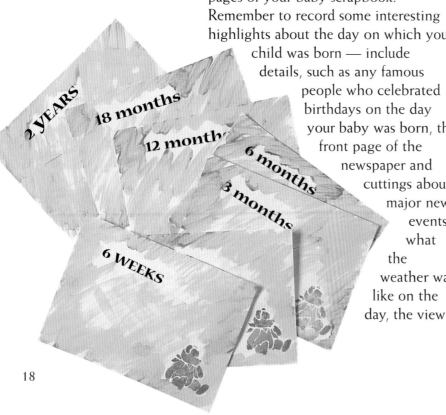

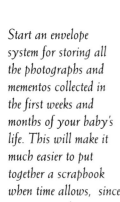

Stamped designs and punched borders can be used to enhance the images in a baby scrapbook.

Start an envelope system for storing all the photographs and mementos collected in the first weeks and months of your baby's life. This will make it much easier to put together a scrapbook when time allows, since you can easily access catalogued material.

of the album cover to highlight the framed image in the center. Stenciled lettering can also be used on the spine of ring binder albums — work BABY or you baby's name on this area. Decorate the cover further with stickers or die-cut shapes.

Instead of working a sampler to hang on the wall, work the details on linen or Aida cloth and use this to cover the album.

There are many details you will want to include in the journaling on the pages of your baby scrapbook. Remember to record some interesting highlights about the day on which your child was born — include details, such as any famous people who celebrated birthdays on the day your baby was born, the front page of the newspaper and cuttings about major news events, what the weather was like on the day, the view from your hospital room, the names of any other mothers and their babies who shared it with you, the room number, what the foreign exchange rates were on the day, and any other details that will be of interest. If you're a sports fan, record the scores and other results of your favorite teams.

When making a record of the christening in the pages of your scrapbook remember to include the recipe for the christening cake, a sample of the fabric used in the christening robe, the pattern and samples or illustrations of any embroidered or smocked details featured on the robe, as well as all the obvious memorabilia, such as cards, a list of gifts, photographs, the service booklet, the invitation and thank-you cards.

A beautifully illustrative way to chronicle your child's development involves taking hand and footprints in paint every few months initially, then every year as they grow older. You could allow two or four pages for recording the prints or just place them

BABY

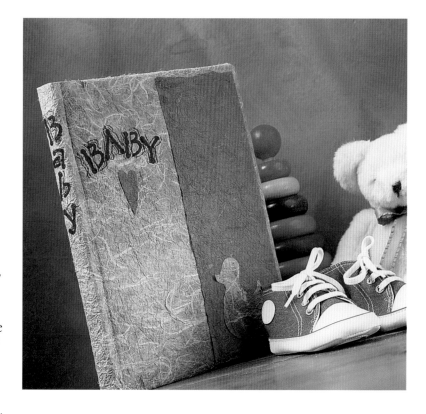

on pages along with photographic images and journaling recording the other developments occurring at the same time. Make a section in which to record your baby's new developments — first smile, first sounds, first tooth, first solid food, first lock of hair or curl, first words, first steps.

Photography can also involve some organization if you are to capture all the memories of the first days and weeks of your baby's life. Write a list of the photographs you would like to include in your scrapbook and make sure you take all these images at the hospital, and later, once you have returned home with the baby. A basic list of photographs will include a record of parent or parents with the baby, siblings with their new baby brother or sister, grandparents with the newest grandchild and any aunts and uncles or special friends with your child. To keep your records updated, make a number of boxes or envelopes, one to record each stage of your baby's life — newborn, six weeks, three months, six months, 12 months, 18 months, then every year after that. This will allow you to keep any images that aren't used in the scrapbook carefully stored for future reference

Some memorabilia can be included to decorate the pages but larger items should be stored in carefully marked boxes. You may wish to trim a large box which will hold the scrapbook and memorabilia or you may prefer to include the pregnancy test result, the ultrasound photograph, your baby's hospital bracelet and some of the cards you received while in the hospital. This memorabilia, along with photographs and journaling that records the baby's weight, time of arrival, the newspaper notice and the names of all that attended the birth, will create a wonderful record for the future.

Cover a baby scrapbook with beautiful handmade rice paper. Use the contrasting colored side to create a striking panel and cut decorative shapes for the front cover, then use markers to work the title.

Baby's Birth

Use these pages to start experimenting with your own scrapbook
designs. Keep in mind that these are merely practice pages, so use
copies of images when creating your pages. The ideas and
inspirations presented in the book will lead you to find your
own unique way in which to present your treasured memories.
Once you have finished experimenting, get started on your first
scrapbook album.

BIRTHDAY

Every birthday is cause for celebration, whether it's a child's special day, a coming-of-age, twenty-first or adult's landmark occasion. Watching the changes that occur as a child grows year by year, or commemorating the birthday of an older relative who reaches the remarkable age of eighty will provide marvelous material for the pages of a scrapbook.

Often it's only the landmark birthdays that are recorded, but don't forget that some of the most memorable events can take place on the less significant birthdays when you capture images of relatives to cherish long after they have passed away, photographs of friends who have since moved away, and many other unexpected surprises that eventuate during the celebrations. You may choose to make a scrapbook of your child's first birthday party or a gift album for a friend turning forty.

Keeping an annual record of birthdays is a project that many parents wish, in hindsight, that they had created for their children. An album such as this can be created at any time, using all the photographs you can gather to highlight the many changes in your child's development.

If planning in advance, make this the scrapbook in which you record all your child's birthdays to be started once the baby album is completed. Save memorabilia associated with children's parties, such as party hats, invitations, acceptances, lists of gifts and party games and favorite recipes prepared for the party, and don't forget to include photographs of special entertainment, such as a clown, magician or pony rides. These can all be used as decorations on the pages along with stamps, stickers, die-cut shapes, stenciled borders, paper shapes traced from templates or your own unique designs.

If making a scrapbook to record all your child's birthdays then try to think of a different theme for each year. Use a diary page showing the day of week on which the birthday falls to introduce each different year. Choose an album that can expand to include extra pages, and plan to feature each birthday over four pages, giving extra space to landmark birthdays.

Collect birthday party memorabilia at the event and use birthday templates featuring cakes and gifts to create your own die-cut shapes which can be used to decorate the pages of your scrapbook.

A record such as this can make a wonderful coming-of-age gift for your child. Birthday cards and other greetings can be incorporated into the scrapbook along with swatches of wrapping paper from gifts, envelopes with interesting stamps from friends, relatives and pen-pals in other countries, birthday cake designs and recipes.

Scrapbooks made for landmark years such as a fortieth or fiftieth birthday make great gifts. If making a book for a special birthday then plan well ahead. Issue everyone at the party with a disposable camera, put them to work recording the event, and don't forget to collect the film at the end of the evening. Ensure all the guests sign the book and ask them to write comments or recount humorous situations or other memorable occasions that they celebrated with the guest of honor. You could also record the menu and any recipes from the party, the music or what the band played in each set, speeches, wine and champagne labels, greetings from those who couldn't attend, and the list of gifts received, or fold up a party hat and place it inside an envelope, complete with streamers, and attach inside the scrapbook cover.

The cover of a birthday album could feature an image of the birthday person

surrounded by decorations or a simple stenciled, stamped or transfer border. Another idea is to cut out paper shapes to represent the number of the birthday, a cake or the shape of a wrapped present. Wrapping paper or colored paper that complements the photograph make a suitable background that can be decorated with ribbons from one of the gifts.

Such a scrapbook makes one of the best gifts to give on a birthday, as the celebration can come to life time and time again.

Wooden albums can be used to great advantage as they can be covered with heavy stock paper, painted or decorated with decoupage and can have a number of pages added to them. Transfers such as flowers and the numeral six and die-cut shapes can be glued onto the cover to complete the effect.

25

Happy Birthday!

SCHOOL DAYS

Many years of our lives are spent at school. During this formative time many experiences occur, both good and bad, some impossible to forget, and all are worthy of being recorded in the pages of a memory album.

Whether you create a scrapbook for each year of your child's schooling or one book that spans all the years, every child will have their own favorite events to record.

School years are more than class photographs and honor rolls — making friends, learning to read and write, visiting exciting locations and participating in fun activities, such as sporting and artistic events, form the highlights of these years, each of which will bring new challenges and achievements.

Parents, teachers and students will have considerably different perspectives on events, so ensure your scrapbook contains comments from them all. What may seem an insignificant event to one may be etched in another's memory. All these accounts will provide entertaining and heart-warming reading in years to come.

Children love to be involved in making their own scrapbooks and may want to take over the organization of their own albums once they are old enough. Your child's memories, written in their own words, will be delightful pieces on which to look back. Ask them to write accounts of their first and last days of school each year, and comments about their friends, teachers, sporting events, school camps, excursions and vacations.

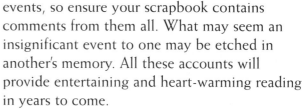

A padded album cover can be created using a ring which as wadding glued in place then covered with fabric. Use fabric from an old school uniform or choose a print that is similar. The padded cover creates a surface on which badges and other school memorabilia can be pinned. Old hair ribbons can be used to trim your photograph, and tied into bows to form pretty decorations.

Children's artwork and poetry can also be featured in the album pages. Encourage them to write down the poems, limericks and rhymes that they have created or enjoyed reading. Perhaps they keep a diary and can search through this to record the highlights of each term or each year on feature pages and choose photographs to accompany them.

Use a collage of photographs to decorate the cover of a school album — these can commemorate everything from stage shows, celebrating Halloween, fetes and fairs, dances or school camp to times spent hanging out with friends. Another idea is to color photocopy a piece of school uniform fabric to use as the background of the cover and a number of feature pages inside the album. You can also cover the album with school uniform or other print fabric, adding wadding behind it for a padded effect. Transfer a photographic image to a contrasting piece of fabric using photo transfer paper or apply a photograph that is backed with acid-free paper, then use the padded background as a pinboard for badges; stitch on buttons from school uniforms and attach favorite hair accessories to make a three-dimensional cover for your scrapbook.

Pages can also be decorated with memorabilia, such as hair ribbons, old library cards, membership cards for school clubs, sporting ribbons, pennants and report cards, along with stickers and die-cut shapes or shapes traced from existing templates or those that you and your child have designed.

Feature pages might include photographs and journaling about a school play or other activity in which your child is involved. Highlight an excellent report card, recount the details of a favorite excursion, or something interesting learned in class.

There will be many materials that can be included in a school album, but it's the unexpected images and decorations that make the greatest impact. What about a collection of pressed leaves and other found objects, salvaged from the pockets of school uniforms just before washing? These little treasures combined with the records of achievements and friendships will result in a delightful school-years' scrapbook.

Use purchased printed papers that are available in a range of different themes, colors and patterns to create interesting backgrounds for your images. Papers presented in book or packaged form are often accompanied by die-cut shapes that highlight the theme and can be used as page decorations ... and don't forget to add your journaling to record all the special memories.

The School Years

GRADUATION

Celebrate a school or college graduation

with a scrapbook that records all the excitement and major events leading up to and on this special day. Scrapbooks such as these can capture the memories of friendships, love and laughter, and all the good times spent at school or college before life takes your child's classmates in different directions.

Keep a record of the grades your child achieved, samples of their projects and essays and take a copy of the graduation certificate on acid-free paper so it can be glued into the scrapbook to become one of its feature pages. They might like to add their own personal comments about their grades and subjects or any areas they particularly enjoyed studying and hope to pursue or perhaps approach teachers and ask them to record their comments in the scrapbook.

As well as writing about study and classes ask your child to write their own list of highlights that occurred during their graduation year and

their hopes and dreams for the future. Capture the excitement of starting the final year, the social occasions that made it a memorable time in their lives and those moments they will cherish for the rest of their lives.

Ideas for the cover of a graduation scrapbook can include the use of a template of a hat and tassel as a mounting board for a class or individual photograph, or ask everyone in the graduation class to sign a sheet of paper to be used as the scrapbook cover over which is positioned a collage of photographs or a focal image. Take copies of the signature sheet before covering the scrapbook as you could continue the theme inside the scrapbook, using this as the background for every alternate page. Ensure you copy the signature sheet onto acid-free paper, and glue plain paper sheets trimmed with paper edgers underneath photographs to provide blank areas for captions.

Ask your child's close friends to create a painted handprint on a piece of paper. These handprints can be placed near their photographs. Invite them to write down how long they have been friends with your child and where they met and put this near the painted print. They may also like to add their own

Use a pre-printed page to form the cover decoration for a Graduation album then add the class photograph, die-cut shapes and lettering to complete the effect.

comments about their graduation year to accompany their photographic images.

One of the other special moments which you will wish to record is the prom night. Allocate two or four pages for this event and include samples of the dress or shirt fabric worn by your child, photographs of them and their partner and friends and the planning involved for this special night. Ask your child to write a record of the date, the venue and how it was decorated, who they took as their partner and include a description of what they wore and the theme of the evening. They might also like to write a short description of the evening's activities and highlights. As well as using die-cut shapes of balloons and streamers as page decorations, there are many stickers available that will complement the prom theme and that can be used to form borders and journaling around photographs.

Major sporting events can also be recorded in a similar fashion. Allow two to four pages for the photographs, program of events and comments, and don't forget to feature the important details, including the score, venue, teams competing and any special training sessions or camps that were held to prepare for the event.

The graduation ceremony itself and any other celebrations that occur on the day should be recorded in the scrapbook. Be prepared for the excitement and make a list of the photographs you wish to take — you and your child, a family shot and one with your child and any siblings, and grandparents, other relatives and friends who attend the ceremony. If giving a special graduation gift to your child, keep a written and photographic record of the event, as well as the wrapping paper used along with other memorabilia from the day, such as the program of events, the order of ceremony and your child's record of memories. These items can be used to decorate the pages of the scrapbook along with photographs, stickers, die-cut shapes and stamped and stenciled designs.

The pages of a graduation scrapbook will come alive with the faces of all your child's contemporaries and the memorable moments that have been captured on film. Encourage your child to be involved in the planning and design of the book as it is one which they will treasure throughout life.

THE BEST GRADUATION PARTY EVER!

FOR: Susie Rose
DATE: 15. 7. 98
TIME: 6 pm
PLACE: Danny's House 16 Elm Drive Ashburton

GRADUATION DAY

I HAD SUCH A FUN DAY ON MY GRADUATION DAY. MUM, DAD, LIT JOSEPH AND LULU CAME ALONG WITH GRAN AND I FELT SO PROUD WHEN I RECEIVED MY CERTIFICATE FROM MRS STEPHANS. LOOKING ACROSS THE ROOM I COULD SEE ALL MY FRIENDS, LOUIE, PATTI, ERNIE AND RICHARD WE HAD SO MUCH FUN. WE THREW ALL OF OUR HATS INTO THE AIR.

The Highlights of My Graduation Day and Year

* Final year party
* Weekend in Hot Springs with my girl friends—Lucy, Mary Lou, Patti and Evie
* My Prom
* Family Graduation Party at the Palm House
* Receiving the "Most Likely to Succeed Award"

Ask your child to write a list of the highlights of their graduation year and day — these can be glued into their scrapbook or used as a reference when compiling the scrapbook.

High School Graduation

This is a scrapbook in which journaling can be used to great effect.

The excitement of purchasing a first car and the independence and freedom that it brings mark it as a special event in everyone's lives. For young adults it's often their first really big purchase and one of the major decisions they will have faced in their lives.

Buying a car is also often associated with the excitement of passing a driving test and making the transition from borrowing and driving the family car every now and then to having all the responsibilities that come with owning such an expensive machine.

Celebrate this major achievement with a scrapbook commemorating the hard work and practice involved in passing the driving test, then the long hours spent looking for the perfect car at the right price. A scrapbook such as this will be most successful when it's planned in advance so you can capture on film the joy of passing the test, gaining the drivers license and securing the sale of the car. And don't forget all the other events in between — the cars that weren't perfect, the days spent driving, walking or catching public transport to find the perfect vehicle. Don't forget to include a shot of the proud owner with the car and any friends or relatives who go along for the first drive.

When making a very specific scrapbook, you can choose a bound album since there will be a limit to the number of pages you want to decorate on this theme. However, if you are thinking about keeping a record of all the cars you or a loved one may own in a lifetime, then a ring-binder album is probably best as it can expand to hold many pages.

A fun-filled page for a first car scrapbook can include a paper cutout car with contrasting wheels and a chequered flag. The journaling can be worked on the car wheels, and a page featuring a photograph of the car can be placed opposite this colorful one.

MY FIRST CAR
Purchased on 20TH MAY 1997

Brrm! Brrmmm! Bbrrmmm!!Brrm!

Today I bought my first car

I was so excited when I signed the papers

A photocopy of the test pass result and the driver's license can be used to decorate the cover of this album or for a simple and graphic design use a colorful paper car shape cut from a template or a purchased die-cut shape and stickers attached to contrasting colored paper.

Include advertisements of cars that were inspected and their photographs, as well as the one finally purchased, the sales document, registration papers, and receipt for the first tank of fuel, then make photocopies of these on acid-free paper so they don't fade. Car stamps, stickers of car accessories and a checkered, hand-drawn, stenciled or paper border around the page will make attractive decorations. Any gifts that the new car owner receives can also be recorded on the album pages in journaling and images.

This is a scrapbook in which journaling can be used to great effect to record the excitement of the event, as well as to highlight the shaped, cropped photographs and decorations. Work the journaling in the shape of a car on one page and glue a photograph on the opposite page, surrounding it with a border of stickers or stenciled or punched shapes. Cutouts made when punching borders and decorative details

can be glued on the pages as well. Any tips that friends and relatives give about maintenance and repairs, as well as the car's specifications, color and previous owners and a list of road rules, can be included in the scrapbook.

You may even consider continuing to take photographs of special events, vacations, good times and outings with friends that involve the use of the car. In this way you will be able to maintain an unusually colorful record book of a car's service.

A simple and effective idea for a scrapbook cover — use colorful stickers such as these ones of traffic lights and road signs, then add embossed lettering to create the focal point of your cover. Simple dots or dashes worked in permanent markers can create a great effect.

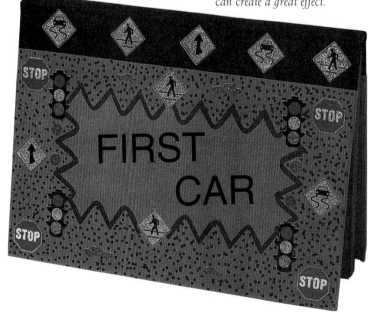

First Wheels

A wedding day is one of the most memorable days in life

— regardless of whether you're the bride, a member of the wedding party, the mother of the bride, a relative or close friend. It's a day filled with precious moments, all of which will provide wonderful material for a wedding scrapbook. The amount of planning and effort that is put into organizing a wedding (months and hectic weeks of preparations) can become some of the aspects you choose to highlight in the pages of your album of memories.

If you are the bride and wish to prepare a book during and after the wedding day then be sure to ask for assistance in gathering and filing material, so nothing is overlooked as the wedding day draws closer. A beautiful gift idea for a bride and groom involves compiling and creating a wedding scrapbook — it will be a unique gift and one that contains much heartfelt preparation.

Decide on the contents of the scrapbook and the order in which each section or chapter will fall. Some of the chapters might include the engagement party, the wedding ceremony and reception preparations, choosing the bridal party attire and designing the wedding dress, the stationery (invitations, place cards, order-of-service booklets, thank-you notes), the wedding shower and kitchen tea party, the

A pretty paper cut photograph border created by using heart-shaped and decorative corner punches forms a beautiful page decoration in a wedding scrapbook. The punched shapes can also be used and can be glued around an invitation or another photograph on the opposite page of the album.

bucks' night and girls' night out, and the wedding day. Do a rough sketch of the number of pages you think should be allocated to each of these then place the material for each section into a separate folder or envelope and label the outside with the name of the section in which the items will feature.

A great filing system or attractive folder can be made from a stack of brown paper bags bound together at one end to create a book. Use cardboard as the front and back covers and to give support to the bags that can be used to store photographs, details of the caterers, florist, dress designer and other contacts for the people involved in making the wedding day a success.

The wedding plans, and even some of those moments when things don't seem to be going according to plan, can all be recorded in your scrapbook. Remember to take a camera along to view reception venues, to dress fittings, the practice makeup and hair sessions, to kitchen and shower teas, and ask your friends for copies of photographs they take during these times. Some of the best memories and images are captured when you least expect them.

When searching for and planning your wedding dress and the attire for the wedding party, keep notes about the shops and designers visited, the fabric and tulle, lace, bead and ribbon samples and any design ideas you gather from magazines or other publications. Don't forget to include the sketches, fabrics and other materials used in the matron-of honor, bridesmaids and other attendants' dresses. All this material can provide the perfect introduction for photographs of the dress and veil fittings and finally, the bride fully dressed on the wedding day.

A wedding scrapbook is also a great place to keep a record of the gifts received, who they were from, the guest list and the acceptances and dates on which they were received. You may also wish to record the table settings and seating arrangements for the reception and keep a copy of the place cards as well as the wedding invitation and thank-you cards.

Exquisite wrapping papers can be used to great effect on the cover of a wedding scrapbook. This cover was covered with a paper that resembles an illuminated manuscript then a plain gold mounting paper was cut with paper edgers to back the photographic image. When using papers such as this, that may not be archival quality, back your photograph with an acid-free paper before attaching it to the mounting paper.

A wedding scrapbook may have a number of different sections, such as the engagement, wedding plans and preparations and wedding day highlights. Think of a theme for the opening pages of each of these sections, then vary the lettering or feature decoration. This album features a paper cast motif that is highlighted with gold ink, stickers and lettering transfers.

The church flowers, scenes outside the church, the booklet that records the service and sheet music copies of the hymns and songs featured during the service can be used to decorate the pages of your wedding scrapbook.

Choosing a color theme and following this throughout the book will result in a beautiful, elegant album. You may like to choose a color from your flowers or one that is featured in the bridal or attendants' dresses, then repeat this on pages throughout the book. Lacy effects can be created by using paper doilies to decorate the edges of pages or use them as stencils and paint a silhouetted image of the doily design onto the pages of the scrapbook. The different chapters of your scrapbook can all feature a similar design. Try to allocate a page as an introduction to each chapter.

Some ideas for decorating the cover of a wedding scrapbook include using a piece of beautiful paper used to wrap a gift, then add a complementary piece of paper as a mounting board for the wedding photograph you have selected to feature on the album cover. Any traditional bridal

mementos, such as a horseshoe, handkerchief or garter, can be added as decoration. Another pretty idea is to cut a white or colored paper border (depending on the color of the album cover) and use this to frame the photograph — this can also create a beautiful page decoration to which little or no journaling need be added. White or gold braid or ribbon can be attached to the cover or spine of the album. Machine embroidered silk or quilted fabric will create a sumptuous cover decoration for a wedding scrapbook. A cover such as this should be well padded with polyester wadding, and gold and white tassels and beaded details can be added for a truly exquisite finish.

Flowers are probably one of the most important elements of the wedding day and one which should be recorded in detail in your scrapbook. While it's impossible to retain the scent, colors and fresh beauty of a wedding bouquet, recording the names of the flower, the colors and varieties that the florist used to created the beautiful arrangements will help to ensure that the memories of those sweet blooms come flooding back each time you open the pages of your scrapbook. Ask the wedding photographer to take a number of photographs of the bouquet alone,

clearly showing all the different flowers and foliage used in the arrangement. Have the florist identify the flowers, giving their common and botanic names. When compiling the scrapbook the flower names can be inscribed on a card or written using calligraphy, then pasted into the scrapbook along with a photograph of the bouquet. The other church flowers, attendants bouquets, grooms and best men's buttonholes, as well as flowers worn by the mother-of-the-bride and other family members, can all be recorded in this way.

As well as recording the types of flowers, the bouquet itself can be dried and framed after the event. Specialist florists freeze-dry the flowers then arrange them in a three-dimensional arrangement in a frame, and others press the flowers then arrange them in a one-dimensional picture. One of the attendants or a friend may volunteer to press the bouquet for you after the wedding day festivities, so the color and scent of the blooms are captured while still fresh. Each flower needs to be pressed between sheets of newspaper and blotting paper which is then placed inside a press. These sheets of paper should be changed daily for the first week, then weekly, while the flowers are still drying.

The pressed flowers can be arranged on a page of your wedding scrapbook to resemble the bouquet arrangement or one of two of the pressed flowers can be positioned with the card identifying each of the flowers. A piece of the ribbon used to tie up the bouquet can also be placed in the scrapbook along with the pressed flowers.

A wedding souvenir box can be made or decorated using fabric, paper, horseshoes, pieces of confetti or dried rose petals, and used to store the wedding scrapbook and any other mementos. You may wish to decorate a series of boxes to be used to store the dress, veil, shoes (and any other attire from the wedding day), the scrapbook, original prints or negatives, mementos, greeting faxes, cards and any other stationery items — and remember to line these boxes with acid-free paper and store them in a cool dark place.

Just as there are many different ways to celebrate, a scrapbook designed to record the occasion will be a unique reminder of the days' celebrations and all that was involved in their preparation.

To store a wedding scrapbook, decorate an acid-free cardboard box with paper, stickers and horseshoes then place the album inside for safe keeping. The album can also be wrapped in acid-free paper for extra protection.

There are all kinds of anniversaries that are worthy of being recorded in a memory scrapbook — wedding, friendship, the date on which long-time partners met, the day a great achievement was realized, and many more occasions that have special personal significance.

When we think of anniversaries many of us recall the number of years a couple has been married, and the anniversaries symbolically grow in importance as the years pass — from paper and tin to silver and gold — from one year to fifty, and beyond.

A scrapbook that gathers together years of memories experienced by a couple is a wonderful gift to give friends and relatives on a special landmark anniversary. Such a scrapbook would record the purchase of their first home, the arrival of the first baby and then its siblings, the vacations, school and church activities, work achievements, and moments just spent enjoying each other's company.

Each of these landmark anniversaries has a traditional theme and you can reflect this in the pages of your scrapbook — use silver, pearl, ruby and gold-colored inks, embossing powders, paper or stenciled images to decorate the pages of an album commemorating 25, 30, 40 or 50 years of marriage. Paper-cut decorations can form attractive mounting boards for images or can be used to create interesting borders on the pages of your scrapbook for a first wedding anniversary, while metal shim decorations can be cut, worked and used as decorative corners for the cover of a tenth (tin) or twenty-fifth (silver) anniversary scrapbook.

If a party is being held to celebrate the anniversary then plan a scrapbook that will incorporate memories from the past as well as images of the party and anniversary day. Plan the number of pages that will be devoted to each of these subjects and don't forget to leave a number of pages on

A simple but striking cover for a 40th wedding anniversary scrapbook is created using two-tone rice paper that has been decorated with plastic jewel beads and glitter paint.

Use metallic paint and metal shim to create a silvery cover for a 25th wedding anniversary scrapbook. Metal shim can be cut to the desired size and embellished by placing the shim on a soft padded surface and then using a sharp pencil or empty ballpoint pen to work the desired design on the wrong side of the shim.

which guests can write their recollections about the couple. Also include the lyrics of favorite songs or poems that have a special significance for the couple. Write these using calligraphy or some creative lettering techniques and use stickers, stencils and stamped motifs to form decorative borders for the pages.

Any floral arrangements the couple receive can also be recorded by selecting a number of flowers from the arrangement and pressing them. These can later be added to the pages of the scrapbook or placed inside or on the cover to form a living decoration. Pressed flowers are best protected with laminating sheets, especially when used on the cover, or create the scrapbook in a ring binder and slip the pages inside protectors to ensure that any pressed material is not lost over time.

As people always have a fascination with family history, a landmark anniversary is the perfect time to draw up a family tree. There are many books about tracing family history available for purchase or try your local library to get started. There is also computer software available that will help you devise a family tree. Once you have the information, draw a tree and add the names or devote one or two pages at the beginning or the end of scrapbook for recording this information. Draw your own large family tree with branches or copy one then add your own embellishments using permanent markers, stickers and small stamped or stenciled designs.

Everyone celebrates anniversaries of special significance at different times during their lives, so mark the occasion by commemorating yours in a scrapbook that allows the memories to be shared with many others in the years to come.

Happy Anniversary

CHRISTMAS

The festive season is a special time, a chance to catch up with friends and family, to gather together to celebrate with good times, food, fun and to give gifts to one another. Each year's celebrations are special in their own way and hold an abundance of memories that can all be recorded in a new scrapbook or in an album that is added to year after year and records the highlights of the season.

A metallic theme has been selected for these pages which celebrate the festive season. The background paper created the most impact so simple decoration is all that's needed. Journaling worked with metallic ink is used to create an interesting effect on the mounting board which backs an oval cropped photograph, while stickers and a paper punched border are used to decorate the photograph on the opposite page.

Keep in mind that your scrapbook should capture the special moments that occur when family and friends (many of whom don't see each other for many months or sometimes even years) gather together — these are some of the most significant memories and they can be captured in images and journaling in the pages of your book.

Remember to label all your photographs with the date and ages of the family members.

Many of the preparations for the festive season can also be recorded in your scrapbook and this will make a wonderful reference for future years — gift and greeting card lists are practical records that can be referred to as each new festive season approaches.

If presented as a beautiful manuscript or with lettering and decorative details, such as stickers and die-cut shapes, they will also make a colorful addition to your scrapbook.

If making a new scrapbook for each Christmas then choose a spiral-bound or cloth- or hand-bound album and plan the space required for each different section. You may like to start your scrapbook with photographs and comments commemorating the hanging

Crushed velvet is used to cover a Christmas scrapbook and gold paper, ribbon and tassel trims are used to complete the theme.

of the tree decorations, then add the guest list for Christmas Day, the greeting cards list (and don't forget to leave room to incorporate a number of the cards you receive), any special recipes for cakes, puddings and eggnog that should be recorded, the dates from the Advent calendar, any drawings or copies of letters to Santa Claus created by your children, the arrival of guests, Christmas Eve and church celebrations, then the Christmas Day festivities. The album can be continued right up until the time of Epiphany (January 6), which is the traditional time to take down the Christmas tree.

Another idea is to allow one or two pages for each family member or close friend and ask them to create their own pages in the scrapbook. Cropping photographs and having them add their own decorative touches and journaling will personalize your scrapbook and record the celebrations from many different perspectives. Some of the more interesting things they might like to record are their secrets for selecting and wrapping gifts, their favorite tree decorations, foods and carols, and fondest memories of Christmases past.

Choose an overall theme for a book that is created to record one year's

Your Christmas card list can be included as part of the Christmas scrapbook and will be an invaluable record in years to come.

With cleverly cropped photographs, a few feature phrases and simple decorations your Christmas scrapbook will come to life.

celebrations, or if keeping an album filled with memories from many different years, select a theme for each year so they are distinctly different; as well, incorporate an opening page commemorating the year and decorate each of these differently. Use felt, paper, stamped or transfer lettering for the numerals and any number of different craft techniques to decorate these pages. Some ideas for themes include using colors (follow a metallic theme using gold or silver and add a color or make a traditional color statement using red or green) or shapes and objects associated with Christmas, such as stars, bells, trees and baubles. Or you might like to go with a sumptuous theme (using velvet and tassels), a country theme (using stencils and natural fabrics)

or a more craft-oriented theme (using quilt and embroidery motifs and fabrics).

Cover ideas can include using a favorite photograph — one of everyone who gathered for the celebration, perhaps one of the tree laden with gifts or one that captures the beauty of the outdoors at this time or year. Velvet can create a sumptuous covering for a Christmas scrapbook and the title and year can be worked in cross-stitch or embroidery on a contrasting piece of fabric or applied directly to the velvet using dimensional fabric paint. Use tassels as the bookmarkers and spine decoration on a book covered in this way. A simple country theme can be created by using hessian or a homespun cotton as a covering for the album. You can create an aged effect by dyeing the homespun cotton with tea or coffee. A border of Christmas motifs can be stenciled around the edge of the cover and the year can be stenciled using a contrasting color. You might also like to add charms, buttons or other plastic or ceramic decorations to this style of cover.

A miniature quilt top or a small quilted or beaded decoration can be

used as the centerpiece for a cover which has a craft theme. Choose a complementary backing fabric then add lettering worked in embroidery thread, fine braid or felt. You may also like to add a photograph and glue this in place on the fabric (remembering to back it with acid-free paper first). Use ribbons or braid to trim the photograph or trace shapes (as you would die-cut ones) but cut them from fabric and add them to the cover decoration.

The pages of your festive scrapbook can be decorated in many different ways. Using paper punches and more than one colored paper to create a two-tone color theme is most effective. Use the punches to create a decorative border for the pages or the photographs' mounting boards. Stencils and transfers can also be used in the same way. Special pages that incorporate material that has been gathered or received, such as Christmas cards, should be carefully planned. A collage of cards is most effective but don't forget to display the greeting part of the cards as well as the image (you may need to cut them in half to do this and this can also add to the collage effect). Your planning list, diagrams of the table setting and seating plans, and a list of the carols

sung by your guests can all be included on the pages of your scrapbook. Any special recipes should be recorded on cards that have been cut and gilded around the edges to create an aged effect. Remember to record the year you first began using them.

Decorations you have made especially for the festive season, such as a wreath of fresh herbs that is left to dry and hung on the front door, embroidered decorations that are made for each family member and friend that attends the festivities, or any other special craft items, should be photographed and the instructions recorded so you and others can carry on the traditions for future Christmases.

Use color to great effect on the pages of a scrapbook that captures the festive season. Colors such as red, blue and green can be used as the page background with extra color added with die-cut shapes and stenciled motifs.

Louisa loved her xmas gift

A Very Merry Christmas

FRIENDSHIP

Friends can come and go

throughout life but some friendships span a lifetime while others, though short, have a great impact on our lives. All these special moments are ones that you might choose to record in a scrapbook to keep for yourself or give to a friend as a birthday gift or commemoration of your friendship anniversary.

Many life-long friendships are formed during childhood, and if you've ever looked back at your own friendships and wished that you had captured those moments, you will want to encourage your children to think of

Use stencils, mounted photographs and stickers to decorate the pages of a scrapbook that celebrates friendships. You may like to write captions for each of the images as you choose them, then add a memento for a sentimental effect.

interesting ways in which they can record these precious experiences. Who is to know just how long a friendship will last, whether it will endure the separation of distance, moving in new circles and interests in different activities? Only time will tell.

If you want to make a gift book for an adult then sort through your old photographs, ask other friends and their relatives whether they have images of your friend that can be included in the scrapbook and, if you have time, plan to take a number of photographs. Ask for annual updates about your friend, their own and family activities and any new interests they have pursued, and include all this information in the album. Change can take place very quickly — within a year they may have moved to a new home, had a new addition to the family, bought a pet, done home renovations, taken a vacation and experienced a number of work achievements, all of which can be included in the scrapbook in images and with journaling.

Over the years you may have collected memorabilia of your friendships — film and theater ticket stubs, letters, photographs of children, birthday cards, papers that wrapped cherished gifts, flowers that you plucked from a fresh bouquet and pressed.

Some of the ideas you might like to encourage children to prepare and preserve include recording their own and their friends' hand and footprints on the pages of their album using acid-free paints. This idea could be repeated every year of their friendship and used as the introduction of the year's activities. Not only is it a different and colorful way to record the changing nature of each of the friends as they grow, it will also be a record of their personal development.

If your child's friend moves away to live somewhere else or they find it hard to be separated during vacation times, then suggest they write letters to each other, recording their thoughts about their friend in verse or prose or capturing the nature of their friendship in a drawing. Poems, favorite music and a list of special shared moments are all ways to record the details of a wonderful friendship.

Friendships will often change in nature as the years slip by, but many friendships withstand the changes brought about by different careers, distance and time, and working on scrapbooks commemorating particular friendships will encourage you to remain in contact with these friends. Maybe you can't attend a special event, such as you friend's wedding or baby's christening, but you can record any thoughts you have on the day and ask your friend to do the same, then use these written commentaries to decorate the page on which you feature the corresponding photographs.

You may also like to highlight any special events of your friendship, such as recollections of the first day you met, your favorite activities, vacations spent together, going to the school prom, graduation, times spent quilting, among many other occasions.

Maybe as you grow older you may like to take an annual photograph of your hands and those of your friend, clasped together, as a way of highlighting the passing of time or send each other annual photographs of yourself and your family. These can then be pasted inside your scrapbook as an addition to your record of friendship.

A collage of photographs looks great in a scrapbook. Mount a number of photographs on a plain page that has a row of punched shapes cut out along the base. Allow the journaling to follow the shapes of the photographs to highlight the collage effect. Choose a patterned paper, a single photograph and simple decorations for the opposite page to create a balanced spread in your friendship scrapbook.

The Best of Friends

The excitement of a first overseas vacation, a honeymoon, family excursion or holiday to an exotic destination are all special events that many of us experience few times in our lives. It is important to record these events in a scrapbook so the memories can be relived over and over again.

Vacation scrapbooks can be planned ahead and assembled once the trip is over, as long as careful planning and storing of mementos has been done during the trip.

When traveling, keep an easy-to-carry journal in which to record your day-to-day activities and any special highlights such as museum and art gallery visits, shopping, sightseeing tours, meals, hotels, restaurants and cafes. Save airline

and entry tickets, coins, postcards and other souvenirs. The best way to store these items is in separate envelopes, marked for each day of your vacation or for each city you visit (these can even be labeled before you leave on your vacation and remember to pack extra envelopes). When all the items have been put inside the envelope, it can be sealed to ensure nothing is lost. When traveling for a number of months, these envelopes can be mailed back to your home at intervals so they do not become too bulky in your baggage.

If traveling on an extended vacation, you may wish to create your scrapbook while you are touring. Take a small kit of scrapbooking tools in a box or soft pencil case (see THE ESSENTIAL EQUIPMENT on page 8) and replenish these as necessary. Aim to work on the scrapbook once a week and allow a few hours to keep the book up-to-date. Use the envelope system but use only one medium or large resealable envelope that can be refilled after each week's addition has been made to your scrapbook.

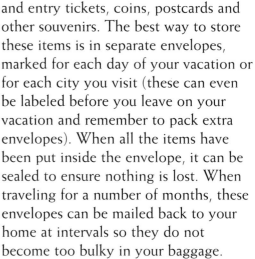

Decorate and label a series of envelopes that will act as files for ticket stubs and other memorabilia collected during a vacation. The envelopes should be clearly marked for each city, country or state visited. A stamped and embossed motif can add a touch of fun to the envelopes. These can be stored along with a portable scrapbooking kit — the essentials for scrapbooking.

You may wish to include watercolor paintings, pastel sketches or cross-stitch and embroidery designs inspired by images and art and craft motifs of the countries visited on your vacation. Local sayings and songs, names of towns and cities, and recipes can all be included in the journaling in your scrapbook pages.

The overall aim of the book should be to capture the highlights of your journey — the unforgettable people and places you visited and the many wonderful memories that were created. Photographs of the people you meet on your journey can be pasted into the scrapbook along with their names and addresses, so the friendships made while traveling can be continued by correspondence when you return home. Don't forget to include the impressions you recorded by senses other than sight — the smells, sounds and emotions that you experienced when visiting different locations should all be recorded and will be powerful tools for recollection when you look at your scrapbook in the future.

Covers for a vacation scrapbook can be decorated in many different ways, but it is best to use one or a series of images that capture the overall impression of your vacation. Make a collage of photographs taken during your vacation with the people you met and the places you visited forming the focus.

Another interesting idea is to cut a postcard or photograph into many different pieces (to resemble a jigsaw puzzle) and then glue these pieces onto the front of your scrapbook, leaving space between each one to create an

Use a postcard you have collected to create this scrapbook cover that looks a little like a jigsaw puzzle. Just cut the postcard into a number of different shaped pieces then glue these over the painted cover of the album to create an exploded effect. Add contrasting colored painted blocks, dots, dashes or other simple designs to finish the scrapbook cover.

Often some wonderful friendships are made during a vacation, so remember to record these in images and words on the pages of your scrapbook — don't forget to write down the postal address of your newfound friend.

Create a memento box for items collected on your travels or with some of the items you plan to store away. Glue ticket stubs, foreign coins, boarding passes and receipts to the outside of a box that is clearly labeled, then place all the other items inside for safe storage.

exploded effect. Paint the cover and spine of the album (if it has one) before gluing the image in place, and choose a color that will create a great background for the photograph or photographs chosen. Border effects can also be created using paint — add different colored stripes, blocks of color, dashes and dots or many other simple effects.

Pages from foreign magazines, train tickets, postage stamps, maps and postcards (and even the bags they are placed in) are some of the many souvenirs that can also be used to illustrate the cover and decorate the pages of a vacation scrapbook. When

decorating a cover with mementos, ensure they are glued securely in place then laminate the entire cover to secure all the layers together and form a protective layer or create a decorated box to protect your scrapbook. Add a pocket inside the lid of the box and use it to store maps or other items that cannot be incorporated into the scrapbook pages.

If using maps to form backgrounds on your scrapbook page, always back any photographs to be glued over the maps onto acid-free paper first to prevent any fading of your precious vacation images. Restaurant reviews of places you have visited can also be included. Try to make each spread of your book a mixture of illustrations and written text. Use city names cut out of travel magazines or from maps to paste onto the pages. Use markers to color the flags of the appropriate countries on the pages or cut out the flags from a map or an old atlas.

Cross-stitch and embroidery designs can also be worked into the cover or placed on the pages of your scrapbook. Use photographs or other images from magazines as a guide to providing the design. You may even wish to make one of these a focal point on a page, framing it with a stamped or stenciled border design.

When creating a vacation scrapbook long after the event, spend time sorting the material you have before you begin. Try to recall any highlights of the trip and record these along with a rough outline of the itinerary. Then use this information as a guide to sorting the material into chronological order. You may wish to search for material from books or magazines or search through postcards at this point to fill in any gaps you have noticed.

Once the material is organized you can choose an album and start planning how the pages are going to look. Do a rough outline for the book, calculating how many pages you will devote to each different city, country or topic. An album such as this can make a wonderful gift for a relative or friend who accompanied you on vacation. You may wish to leave spaces for them to add their own journaling on the pages or you may want to consult with them before writing in the scrapbook.

If you are planning to give the album as a gift, then make or decorate a box that will form a decorative and protective cover for your scrapbook and reflect the contents inside. You may also like to include a few of the extra mementos you have saved from your vacation and which could not be incorporated into the scrapbook. Line the box with acid-free paper and wrap each memento in paper or place inside a clearly labeled envelopes to ensure they are safely stored away.

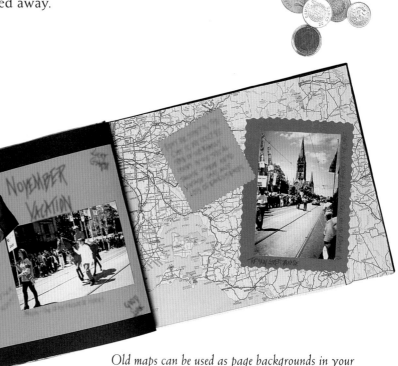

Old maps can be used as page backgrounds in your vacation scrapbooks, and you may even wish to plot the routing of your holiday to keep as a reference.

Where in the World?

Houses become part of the family and many important family events are played out inside their walls. So when moving from one home to the next or when purchasing your first home, it's important to preserve the memories of special times and record all the experiences associated with settling into the new property.

The excitement of a new home is often overshadowed by the time and effort that goes into finding and purchasing it and then into moving. It's so easy to forget to overlook the importance of keeping a photographic record of these times — images that will help you recollect these experiences long after you're comfortably settled in.

If it's the first home you've ever owned then create a scrapbook especially for this occasion. If you plan to include records of any other houses you may move to later, choose an album that's expandable. If you're creating an album for a friend or relative who has bought a new home, then opt for one that is bound.

Cover a scrapbook for a new home with leftover furnishing fabric. Add braid and felt letters to create the trim, then slip photographs of your home underneath the braid.

Take some time to organize your thoughts about what you'd like to include and always keep your camera ready at hand to capture all the impromptu moments of fun and chaos as they unfold.

Record the home after the purchase and before you move in — take photographs of it with the SOLD banner displayed and from different angles outside. When it's empty photograph the inside as this will be an invaluable record if you're planning to renovate. Write down your personal experiences about the purchase, how the house looked when you first inspected it and what made you buy it, as well as your thoughts on moving in and deciding where to place the furniture.

Draw a floor plan of how the home looked when you bought it or moved in; record how much you paid and whether you bought it at auction or by sale, the interest rate at the time and the monthly payments. All these details can be included in the colorful journaling that accompanies your photographs and is used to enhance these images.

There are many other items of memorabilia as well as photographs that can be saved and used as cover or page decorations in your scrapbook. Remember to include the estate agent's brochure as well as your initial ideas for renovations and extensions, then add the final plans. Leave a number of pages at the end to record any other changes you may make during the time you live in the home. This could include photographs taken each time you make improvements, a written record of what you planted in the garden, your neighbors throughout the years, color swatches of the different paint shades and fabrics used throughout the home and any animals and additions to your family that came along while you lived in this home.

Include photographs of the house warming party if you plan one, any gifts received, the guests who attended and the recipes for the hors d'oevres and cocktails that were served. You may also like to include images and memorabilia from some of the special occasions celebrated in your home — the birth of a child, the visits of old friends, the arrival of a new puppy or kitten.

To make a beautiful and accurate record of your home draw, embroider or cross stitch a picture on paper, linen or Aida cloth, and use contrasting fabric to form a border or frame it and secure this framed picture onto your album cover. Acid-free wadding can be glued on to create a slightly padded effect. To create

a more simple cover use leftover furnishing fabrics or paint then decorate the cover with a collage or photo images or a mixture of photographs and memorabilia and cutouts from felt or use die-cut shapes to form the number of your house and glue these numbers in place on the cover.

A home should be a place of stability and comfort where all the family can unwind and enjoy the many good times they spend together, so keep this in mind when planning and creating your scrapbook, and ensure that it captures some of these special moments and memories.

Plans of the home as it was when you bought it, photographs that were taken before renovations began, and your plans and ideas for improvements can all be used in the pages of a scrapbook that highlights the transformation of your home.

Home Sweet Home

When creating a scrapbook to commemorate a special musical achievement or performance, photocopy the musical score and use this to form the background of the cover. Black velvet ribbon can be used as the trim.

There are many occasions in life that are worthy of being recorded in a scrapbook, but some of the most precious are those shared with your children. Their excitement when succeeding at a major event or attaining that achievement toward which they have been striving for so long — passing a piano exam, winning a public speaking competition or triumphing at a sporting event — is an important occasion that can be commemorated in a memory scrapbook.

Along with all the photographs you will have taken to record the event, other items such as reports, certificates, ribbons, medals, prize cards and programs can also be incorporated into the book to make it a living memory of the event.

Whether planning in advance or working with materials at hand after the event you will also find much that can be used decoratively and introduce other effects by means of die-cut shapes, stamps, stickers, patterned papers and other accessories that are readily available to be used to brighten the pages and complement the photographs and memorabilia.

If you can plan ahead, take shots at practice sessions, rehearsals and during all the other preparatory events. Take group photographs of the team, choir, or orchestra of which your child is a member.

If there is a printed program available that outlines the event, buy at least two — one to store away (you can create a pocket at the back of the album for this) and one to cut up for the cover or feature pages of your book. Decorative ideas could include having the other members of the group sign a page of the book or record their signatures or comments by writing them around the groups' photographs. If a sporting event, maybe they can sign a shirt, jersey or prepared piece of paper that can later be photographed and recorded in the book. Take photographs of the trophy or prize with and without the successful team or performer holding it and paste these in the book too.

An item of clothing such as a uniform can even be used to form part of the cover decoration. Cut a piece from the garment or use the whole thing. Fabric can be decorated in a number of ways — use dimensional fabric paints to write words directly onto the fabric, or stencil motifs and letters into the fabric using acrylic paints. If you don't want to use a garment or fabric to cover the scrapbook then another alternative is to take a color photocopy of the fabric and use this to cover the book, then decorate it with the corresponding jersey or player number and the position played, and store the item of clothing safely away.

Keep a record of the date of the event, the location or venue and make these important details features on the cover or inside the scrapbook. To use them to great decorative effect on the cover, cut out the letters and figures from colorful paper and glue them onto a contrasting colored or patterned background around the focal image on the cover — the photograph of the triumphant individual or team. A nice cover idea for a book that highlights a musical event is to copy the score or use the original to form the album cover. The dates and other details can be drawn, cut out and attached to the score to create great effects. Use black velvet ribbon to trim the cover and spine.

Reports, rosettes, ribbons, lucky swimming caps or charms, and similar items of memorabilia can be used to decorate the cover or laminated using acid free sheets and attached to the scrapbook. Other pages might feature the words of the team song, copies of poems performed, a transcript of a speech delivered or quarter and halftime scores of a game of basketball, net ball or football.

Mementos can also be stored away with a scrapbook, wrapped in paper or placed inside envelopes. Remember to record when the mementos were received or bought giving the date, the special occasion and any other relevant information that will help you recollect the experience in the future.

Ribbons, pennants, medals, rosettes and other memorabilia need not be stored away but can be used to decorate the cover or pages of a scrapbook.

A Great Achievement

INDEX

acid-free papers and equipment
    8–9, 11, 13
albums
    acid-free 11
    types of 7, 8, 11
    wooden 24
anniversaries 48–51
artistic achievements 76–79
artwork, children's 29

baby's birth 16–23
binders 7, 8, 11
birthdays 24–27
bouquet 43
boxes
    choosing 11
    for photographs 10, 11
    for vacation memorabilia 66
    for wedding souvenirs 43

calligraphy 49
car, first 36–39
cardboard boxes 10, 11
cards
    Christmas 54, 55
    vacation 65–66
children
    artwork by 29
    baby scrapbook 17
    birthday scrapbook 24–27
    friendship scrapbook 60, 61
    poetry by 29
    sporting or artistic
        achievement scrapbook 76
christening 16–23
Christmas 52–59
collage of photographs 61
color
    baby scrapbook 17
    Christmas scrapbook 54, 55
    of photographs 14
    wedding scrapbook 42
country theme 54
covers
    baby scrapbook 17
    birthday scrapbook 24
    Christmas scrapbook 54–55
    decorating 12
    graduation scrapbook 32
    padded 28
    quilted 54–55
    school scrapbook 28, 29
    sporting achievement
        scrapbook 76–77
    vacation scrapbook 65–66
    wedding scrapbook 42
cropping photographs 12, 13, 14

decorations
    Christmas scrapbook 55
    covers see covers
    school day scrapbook 28
    sporting or artistic
        achievement scrapbook 76
die-cut shapes 9
drivers license 36–37

edgers 9
embossing
    lettering 37
    tool 9
engagement party 40, 42
envelopes 11, 13, 64
equipment 8–9

fabrics
    decorating 77
    uniforms 28, 29, 76–77
family tree 49
floor plans 72, 73
flowers
    anniversary 49
    wedding 42
focal point 12, 13
folders 11
footprints 18
friendship 60–63

gifts
    baby scrapbook 17
    birthday scrapbook 24
    friendship scrapbook 60
    graduation scrapbook 33
    vacation scrapbook 67
glue 8
grades, school 32
graduation 32–34

handprints 18, 32
hanging files 11
home, new 72–74

ink pads 9

journal, travel 64
journaling 15
    baby scrapbook 18
    effects 13
    first car scrapbook 37

labeling photographs 10
lacy effects 42
lettering
    anniversary scrapbook
        49
    embossed 37
    in journaling 15

maps 66, 67
markers 9
memorabilia
    baby 19
    birthday 24
    boxes for see boxes
    friendship 60
    mounting of 13
    new home 72–73
    school day 28
    sorting of 10
    sporting or artistic
        achievement 77
    use of 6
    vacation 65–66
    wedding 41
metal shim decorations
    48, 49
motherhood 16–23
mounting boards 12, 14
mounting tapes 8

objects see memorabilia

padded album covers 28
page protectors 8, 11
pages for binders 8
paints 8
paper
    pre-printed 28, 32
    types of 8
    wrapping 41
paper bags, bound 41
photograph corners 8
photographs
    baby 19
    border for 42
    boxes for 10, 11
    choosing 13–14
    Christmas 53, 54
    collage 61
    color scheme 14
    cropping of 12, 13, 14
    first car 37
    friendship 61
    journaling of see journaling
    mounting of 12–13
    new home 72, 73
    school days 28
    silhouetting of 14
    sorting of 10
    sporting achievements 76
    wedding 41, 42
plan of new home 72, 73
poetry, children's 29
post-bound albums 7, 8, 11
postcards 65–66

pre-printed paper 28, 32
pregnancy 16
presents see gifts
programs 76
prom night 33
punches 8–9, 55
quilted cover 54–55
report cards 28
rice paper 19
ring binders 7, 8, 11
rubber stamps 9

school days 28–31
school graduation 32–34
scissors
    decorative 9
    types of 8
scrapbooking centers 11
shelving 10, 11
silhouetting photographs 14
sorting material 10
souvenirs see memorabilia
spiral-bound albums 8, 11
sporting achievements 33,
    76–79
stamps 9
stencils 9, 55
stickers
    availability of 9
    first car scrapbook 37
    in journaling 15
storage
    methods of 11
    on vacation 64

tapes, mounting 8
templates 9
themes
    baby scrapbook 17
    birthday scrapbook 24
    Christmas scrapbook 52,
        53–54
transfers 9, 55
traveling 64

uniform fabrics 28, 29, 76

vacation 64–72

wedding 40–46
wooden albums 24
wrapping papers 41